To John and Joan
on your Retirement
June 25, 1995

From Bonnie and Eileen

You have guided and challenged us
Believed in and encouraged us
Laughed and cried with us
You have left "footprints on our hearts
And we will never be the same
God Bless You Both

Flavia

Footprints On Our Hearts
copyright © 1993 by Flavia Weedn
All rights reserved. Printed in Hong Kong.

For information write Andrews and McMeel,
a Universal Press Syndicate Company,
4900 Main Street, Kansas City, Missouri 64112

ISBN: 0-8362-4707-8

FOOTPRINTS
ON OUR HEARTS

Written and Illustrated
by Flavia Weedn

Some

people

come into

our lives

and

quickly

go...

like

an

ocean

wave

when

it

touches

the shore...

or a

cloud

that is there

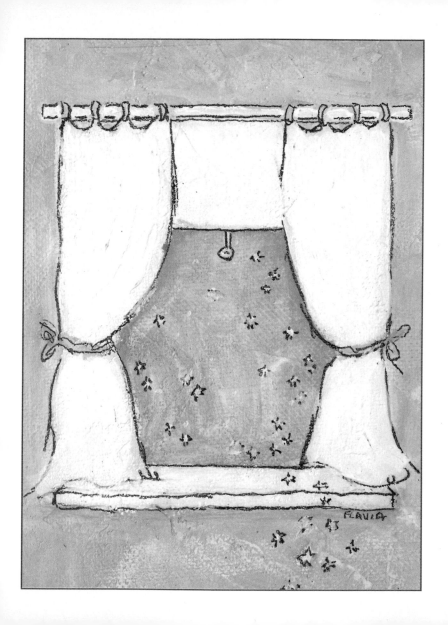

and

then

gone.

Some

people

stay for

a while

and

although

we may be

unaware

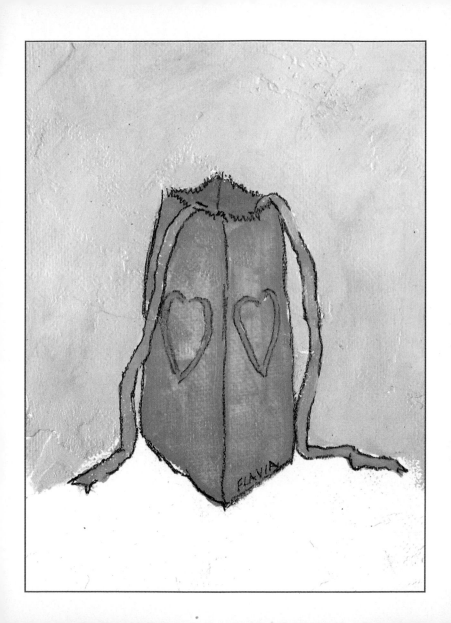

they are touching

our lives in

a special way.

When they

are gone,

it is then

we understand...

they

have left

footprints

on our hearts

and we will

never, ever

be the same.

That

is

when

we know...

blessed

are

we.

Flavia at work in her Santa Barbara studio

Flavia Weedn is a writer, painter and philosopher. Her life's work is about hope for the human spirit. "I want to reach people of all ages who have never been told, 'wait a minute, look around you. It's wonderful to be alive and every one of us matters. We can make a difference if we keep trying and never give up.'" It is Flavia's and her family's wish to awaken this spirit in each and every one of us. Flavia's messages are translated into many foreign languages on giftware, books and paper goods around the world.

To find out more about Flavia write to:
Weedn Studios, Ltd.
740 State Street, 3rd Floor
Santa Barbara, CA 93101 USA
or call: 805-564-6909